D1488116

The
AMERICAN COUNTRY
Companion

The
AMERICAN COUNTRY
Companion

Judith and Martin Miller

CollinsPublishersSanFrancisco

A Division of HarperCollins*Publishers*

First published in USA in 1994 by
Collins Publishers San Francisco
1160 Battery Street
San Francisco CA 94111

Library of Congress Cataloging-in-Publication Data

Miller, Judith.
    The American country companion / Judith and Martin Miller
            p.   cm -- (Country companion series)
        Includes index.
        ISBN 0-00-255367-8
        1. Decoration and ornament, Rustic--United States. 2. Interior
    decoration --United States--History--20th century. I. Miller,
    Martin. II. Title. III. Series.
    NK2004.M56   1994
    747.213--dc20   93-28954
                                                  CIP

First published in 1994 by Mitchell Beazley,
an imprint of Reed Consumer Books Limited,
Michelin House, 81 Fulham Road, London SW3 6RB
and Auckland, Melbourne, Singapore and Toronto

Photography by James Merrell
Illustrations by Claire Melinski

Text and design Reed International Books Limited Copyright © 1994

Produced by Mandarin Offset
Printed and bound in China

CONTENTS

Introduction

American country style is the style of an independent people. It developed from native Indian ingredients that were blended with a rich seam of traditions and skills imported from Europe by the early pioneers, who built their homes with whatever materials came to hand. This melting pot of old and new was stirred until a style evolved that was distinctively American, yet evocative of its pioneer roots. The isolation of the pioneering communities from each other produced a variety of strong regional styles, from that of the Ohio farmhouse set among the midwest's rolling plains to the Cape Cod cottage perched by the sea.

9

What American country styles have in common is an
abundance of wood, from the Atlantic's white cedar to the
cypress of the deep south. Like farmers all over the world,
the settlers built homes using the resources they found, but
with the difference that, as transposed people, they were
influenced by the traditions of their original countries or
by the religions that they carried with them like baggage.
By applying the criteria of what was natural, comfortable
and would last, rural folk created their own classics of
interior design and furnishings, based on the fundamentals
of simplicity and a love of fine craftsmanship.

The modest cabin was a typical pioneer home. The dimensions of such dwellings were largely determined by the height of the trees — and therefore the length of the logs that they yielded — found in the vicinity. Many log cabins were constructed without windows.

Choosing a Style

An abiding symbol of the pioneering spirit, the humble log cabin enshrined the virtues of rustic living. It was built from rough-hewn logs that were chinked in winter to protect against the cold and ventilated in summer by warm breezes. With the advent of sawmills, many log dwellings were covered with weatherboards to raise their status. In the northeast, early colonial houses were wooden frame structures, characteristically built around an enormous central chimney. As agriculture took a hold and farms increased in size, shingled barns – raised by a handful of people within a day – became a feature of the landscape across central America. In the south, large, white-painted plantation houses were designed to resemble the lines of classical temples and reflect the status of the resident landowner. While homes in northern climes were designed to retain heat, the warm climate of the south made keeping cool a priority so balconies, porches, large windows and high ceilings were the norm.

Old walls of planks, logs and tongue-and-groove,
whether painted or left bare, lend warmth to a room.

Above: Strong, earthy colors
set off a whitewashed wall.
Left: A colonial country room
with green milk paint walls
and a Windsor chair.
Right: An 18th-century New
England blanket chest.
Opposite: Open fires will give
paintwork an aged look and
an attractive patina.

Alongside the original log cabin, early American dwellings consisted of homes which were adapted to the practical considerations of climate and locally available raw materials. Colonists in the northeast built a variety of houses based on familiar European forms. The style of the New Englanders on the east coast was colored by the tones of England. For example, the classic Cape Cod cottage was modeled on the stone-built single-room English cottage, complete with dormer windows and a gabled roof, but it was then modified to meet the conditions of the eastern seaboard of America. One side of the gable roof might be swept down, in what became known as the saltbox house, in order to help fend off the northerly winds. And instead of England's stone and clay, the settlers had to work with Atlantic white cedar, from which they cut shingles to tile their facades and roofs, or clapboards, which weathered to a silvery gray in the coastal climate. Likewise, the interiors of the Cape Cod cottages conjured up the gentle tones of England: the matchboarded walls were painted in soft colors – buff, cream and gray-green. The ground-hugging saltbox houses were insulated with clay and straw and featured small window openings and low ceilings

to retain heat efficiently during the long winter months. Such simple and austere designs provided appropriate surroundings for the rural compounds created by the Puritans, the Quakers, the Huguenots, the Amish and the Shakers. It is perhaps the modest interiors created by these religious communities that are the most famous and most loved of rural styles from America. The strict creeds that governed their hearts and homes resulted in a strong style that is so utterly simple that it looks almost modern.

As settlers established themselves in the hope of reaping a living from the land they built dwellings to accommodate the many requirements of a working farm. Many farmhouses were made up of numerous adjuncts, for instance the springhouse enclosed a spring or a brook for cooling milk and other fresh products; the smokehouse was for salting and smoking meat; the icehouse contained blocks of ice cut from nearby lakes and acted as a primitive type of refrigerator; the woolhouse was given over to spinning, weaving and stitching sheeps' wool. In addition a wellhouse, a washhouse, a root cellar and a woodpile were commonly found on farmsteads.

From the mid-19th century onward, New England farmhouses were built around timber or "balloon" frames using plentiful supplies of local oak and then weatherboarded. Although simpler in style than most town dwellings, they were influenced by the so-called Victorian style and acquired fancy carved trimmings such as decorative gingerbread trim.

Indoor life revolved around a huge, walk-in fireplace, which, although smoky and inefficient, radiated heat throughout the house and was used for cooking and heating water. With improved flue designs, fireplaces became smaller, less smoky and a feature of most rooms. Interiors were furnished with simple homemade essentials and perhaps the occasional family treasure such as a Bible or some brass candlesticks.

Left: The Tullie Smith house is an unadorned plantation farmhouse dating from the 1840s. There are sturdy brick chimneys at each end of the building and a typical southern veranda. It is preserved by the Atlanta Historic Society.
Right: Typical of a colonial interior, this simply decorated house brings economy to the fore. The hall room was the main living area of the house and is furnished with a collection of 19th-century furniture from the southern states. The open doors of the 18th-century style corner cupboard reveal pottery decorated with American scenes.

BARN

Most old barns are built of horizontal log construction and held together by notches and pegs at each corner. As adjuncts to farmhouses, their purpose was to shelter animals, crops and agricultural machinery. The walls were chinked with strips of fabric or an infill of mud and unhewn or round logs could be square-hewn to give interior walls a close-fitting, flat surface. The exterior of the barn was often shingled, which served to conceal and weatherproof the logs underneath and at the same time insulate the interior.

The component parts of the structure were felled from surrounding trees, cut, hewn and assembled. Then, under the command of the barn builder and with the help of willing local hands, horses or oxen, it was raised into position.

A lower floor, often made of masonry, housed the farm animals and above this a floor made of wood (where the logs were left unchinked to allow ventilation) provided ample space for storing hay to feed them. Barns sometimes retain a pulley high up in the roof area – a reminder that bales were once hauled up from a wagon on the ground to replenish the supply in the loft.

Some barns, particularly in Wisconsin, were constructed by the stovewood method developed by Canadian lumberjacks. This type of barn is so-called because quantities of wood cut small enough to fit into a stove were stacked tightly and held together with lime mortar, so forming a wall. The exterior was shingled or clapboarded and the interior was often plastered.

Left: A collection of architectural stars, *fleur de lys*, tie rods and eel spears decorate a large expanse of barn wall. The painted furniture has been collected from all over North America. Each painted cupboard has a different origin – Canada to the left, New Hampshire to the right and Pennsylvania in the middle. A decoy duck sits on a brown-stained table from New York State and a green ladderback chair originates from New England.
Right: A Maine connected farmhouse consisting of big house, little house, back house and barn.

COWBOY

The popularity and cult status of the cowboy lives on, for he is a potent symbol of freedom and the great oudoors.

When the craftsman and designer Thomas Molesworth began to produce his unique ranch-style arts and crafts furniture in Cody, Wyoming during the 1930s, he truly defined the tough, rugged, masculine and quintessentially American cowboy style. And in so doing he elevated the legends of the Wild West, along with their strong element of fantasy, to an art form that expressed the lost dreams of a nation.

Molesworth's furniture was distinctive and decorated pictorially. He painted and stenciled chests of drawers, chairbacks, friezes on bedheads and bed-ends, rawhide lampshades and even drapes in a harmonious mixture of Indian motifs and artefacts – bows and arrows, canoes and feathered headdresses – with classic cowboy imagery such as silhouettes of bandy-legged gunslingers, 10-gallon hats, bucking broncos, stetsons, saddles and spurred boots. While cowboy-style cupboards, chests and tables are typically painted or carved with Western images,

Left: The living room of this Colorado ranch, designed in 1935, is a shrine to Thomas Molesworth, who defined cowboy style.
Above: A chunky carved coffee table stands in front of a macho leather couch displaying 1930s Chimayo weavings from New Mexico.
Right: A classic Molesworth interior contains furniture decorated with cowboy imagery.

couches and chairs are a heavy, macho blend [of] wood and leather or animal hide, with perha[ps a] token "frill" in the form of leather fringing. [A] natural burl in wood – a benign tumor on a [tree] which gives branches or trunks a misshapen [look] – can be cut through horizontally and then i[ncor]porated in the design of, for example, a table [or] stool top to handsome effect. Materials taken

Above: Cowboy boots and hats are appreciated for their decorative qualities and make an original mantel shelf display.
Right: A carved frieze of horses' heads and a gunslinger silhouette embellish a chest of drawers in a bedroom. Colored leather and a fringe of leather tassels typify Molesworth's style of furniture.

Right: A giant *saguaro* [cac]tus, a stetson hat and [a] native American blan[ket] are all characteristic [of] cowboy-style interior[s;] sepia photographs on [the] wall document dying [?] from the late 1800s.
Below: A pair of polish[ed] cowboy boots and a Wyoming candlestick [?] set against the backdr[op of] a hanging Navajo blan[ket.]

of their natural context are brought indoors for decorative purposes. Twigs, moose antlers and cow or buffalo horns fashioned into chairs, small tables, chandeliers, candlesticks, hat stands, hooks and lamps all serve to emphasize the cowboy's love of the outdoors and lend a rough, homespun quality to the surroundings. In order to complete this close affinity with the landscape a giant *saguaro* cactus, a fertile symbol of the arid plains, will strike an authentic note.

22

Although the style eschews the need for any superfluous comfort and sophistication, and walls, ceilings, floors, doors and furniture are predominantly made of wood, color is an important part of the overall effect. Red, blue or white leather upholstery, or perhaps some gingham draped across a window or over a table are in keeping. However, it is above all the colors and patterns of native American weavings and blankets which lend these interiors warmth and a welcome touch of rustic cosiness. Traditional Navajo, Beacon and Pendleton blankets may be hung on the walls, over banisters or else draped over furniture or used as bed covers, and rugs break up the monotony of floorboards.

Left: In a Santa Fe home a magnificent full-length Assinabo feathered headdress from the northwest coast is displayed above the carved wooden bench which once belonged to the same Indian chief.

Right: An impressive fireplace constructed from smooth river boulders which cover the height of the chimney breast. The use of rocks is a reminder of the native American fondness for incorporating nature into design. The bleached skull with horns above the open fire and the *kiva* ladder on the left are typical features of Santa Fe homes. The rungs of the ladder provide a perfect framework for displaying Pendleton blankets. In the foreground are a native American basket and pair of slippers.

Native American culture has had a deep and lasting influence on the country's ethnic design. The southwest corner of the United States is the cradle of the arts and crafts of ancient civilizations and in this region Indian artefacts blend comfortably with the grander and more ornate Spanish colonial style.

Against a sun-baked landscape early dwellings were molded from the arid terrain. Adobe (the Spanish-American name for a brick made of earth and hardened by the sun) was a prime building material. While still wet it was shaped into smooth arches, curving walls and rounded fireplaces usually set into the corner of the room.

From the 1930s onward Santa Fe became an artists' colony. In today's houses the original dirt floors have given way to cool brick or flagstones, although ceilings copied from original structures and supported by pine-log rafters are reminders of the Indian pueblo tradition. Other typical features of these interiors are the bleached animal skull and the *kiva* ladder. The *kiva* was an underground chamber accessible only by ladder and a meeting place for men. Today the *kiva* ladder is a prized possession and provides a suitable means of displaying traditional rugs and blankets.

Set against the faded earthy tones of these interiors which reflect the hues of the desert environment, it is the rich array of native American arts and crafts which unfailingly catch the eye. In addition to glittering beadwork and jewelry, tribes such as the Cherokee and the Pima twined baskets from hazel, willow, grass, oak, ash and hickory and turned animal hair, cotton, milkweed, hemp and wood fibers into textiles. The Hopi tribe wove vivid cloths and soft-hued blankets on simple belt looms made from sticks. Likewise, brilliantly striped Navajo rugs and red and black Indian pottery decorated with geometric shapes and stylized animals or birds are today's valued collector's pieces.

Tex-Mex is a confident fusion of the relatively grandiose Spanish colonial influences and the more naive decoration characteristic of indigenous Indian cultures. In defiance of a somewhat dusty and colorless world outside this is an extrovert southern style where rich designs and bold colors are traditionally applied to all kinds of surfaces including tiles, pottery, ceramics, rugs, textiles, walls and furniture.

Constructed in the main from organic materials, rooms feature log-beamed ceilings, flagstone floors, wooden door and window frames and adobe-style arches and corner fireplaces.

Walls are coated with smooth stucco and painted white or a pale shade of pink, blue, yellow, buff or green. These cooling pastel backgrounds set off a multitude of ornamental accessories, for example, religious and pagan ephemera, painted figures, silver-tin mirrors and picture frames and, in the kitchen, decorative collections of beaten or punched tin receptacles. Inspite of heavy, wood furniture an overall cheerfulness is expressed through vivid paintwork. In particular the bright blue or *azul anil*, once believed to ward off evil spirits, lends an authentic touch if used to pick out architectural details.

Left: Through a wide adobe archway lies an elegant, almost ecclesiastical dining room with a primitive chandelier above the table and a delightful mismatch of old Mexican chairs.
Top right: An adobe-style fireplace traditionally set into a corner, is decorated with a trio of crucifixes *(left)*. Aged wood-work and thick painted earthenware create a homey peasant feel *(middle)*. A large religious painting dominates an entrance hall *(right)*.
Bottom right: Traditional Mexican dining-room chairs together with heavy wooden doors, window frames and shutters complement the narrow-beamed ceiling and the dark paintings on the walls. A chair upholstered in bright Navajo weaving adds a note of color.

*I*n the late 19th century, as a reaction to rapidly expanding urbanization coupled with the growth of industry, a back-to-nature movement grew up in America that sought to fulfill the yearning for a return to pioneer roots. The result was the emergence of rustic-looking Adirondack log cabins. Ironically perhaps these were not authentic rural homes, nevertheless they were certainly inspired by the country idyll.

In the far north of New York state Adirondack camps were created as weekend summer retreats where wealthy city dwellers could temporarily turn their backs on life in the metropolis. Today, an open-air museum which preserves Adirondack pioneer-style dwellings can be visited at Blue Mountain Lake. Throughout wood is the predominant material used for the construction of walls, floors, ceilings and

Right: This rustic-style table with a twisted root base dates from c.1900. It was made for an Adirondack cabin at Raquette Lake in New York State. North American Adirondack furniture makers were well known for incorporating all sorts of organic forms into their designs. In addition to tree roots, branches, twigs and many different types of bark were used to striking decorative effect.

Top right: The living room of Bull Cottage at Blue Mountain Lake which forms part of the Adirondack Museum. The furniture was made by a carpenter called Ernest Stowe.
Middle right: A pair of yellow birch rocking chairs with woven ash splint backs and seats.
Bottom right: The decorative qualities of bark are enormous: sometimes as many as ten types are used in a single piece of furniture.

furniture. Designers took the original furnishings of real log cabins – basic shapes made from bent boughs and notched woods – to an extreme in order to create a look of exaggerated rusticity. Rough-hewn furniture made by local craftspeople incorporated the natural forms and irregular shapes of the raw material and so provided the perfect complement to peeling log beams, exposed wooden ceilings and stone fire-places. Carpenters made the most of the decorative qualities of bark, creating a variety of wood effects: a server or cup-board might be inlaid with white birch bark and split yellow birch rods, a chest of drawers covered with ornate bark marquetry and a table or a cabinet high-lighted with fancy twig patterning. Wood was not only heavily applied but also woven. For example, ash and hicko-ry splints were woven into the backs and seats of rocking chairs.

Organic forms such as branches, roots and twigs were integrated into furniture designs. For instance, boughs were bent into curved head- and footboards for beds; lamp bases were fashioned from sections of tree trunks felled from the surrounding forests; antlers were turned into hooks or candle-holders and a stool might sit upon four deer hoofs.

SHAKER

*L*ed by an Englishwoman, Ann Lee, the Shakers were one of a number of Utopian sects which migrated to the New World. They arrived in 1774, and within a decade had established their central community in New Lebanon, New York State. In their heyday, around the middle of the 18th century, as many as 6,000 Shakers lived in communities as far west as Ohio. Mother Anne's exhortation to her followers: "Do your work as though you had a thousand years to live and were to die tomorrow", goes a long way to explaining the fine craftsmanship, perfect design and inherent usefulness of Shaker products.

Since a Shaker interior doubled as a meeting place it needed to be as uncluttered as possible. In general, the walls

Above left: Original red paintwork on a Shaker cupboard.
Above right: Pegs keep kitchen brushes out of the way.
Below: A "stairway to heaven" of colorful storage boxes.

were painted in clear, soft colors, the windows were left bare and wooden floors were highly polished. Small objects were packed away in round wooden boxes, painted in reds, blues, yellow and greens to color-code their contents. And garments, tools, kitchen utensils and even chairs were hung on pegboards fixed to the walls in order to retain a sense of order which created a feeling of almost monastic calm.

Left: Contemporary Shaker furniture is well-crafted and has a timeless elegance.
Below: The "curly" or tiger maple ladderback side chair and tripod table date from c.1850. The candlestick design was first seen c.1750 and was still being produced in the 1920s. The sewing basket is mid-19th-century. The wide planking and soft but strong green color on the walls are in typical Shaker style.

The Great Outdoors

In 1850, the architect A. J. Downing compared one of his designs for a traditional American farmhouse with a similar one in the English rural style. He wrote: "There is perhaps in this house a little more independence and a little less lowliness manifested, both being expressed in the higher stories and the greater space from the ground to the eaves in this design." It would appeal to American farmers, he added, because they "love independence above all things." Wherever the pioneers came to establish their roots within the vast open spaces of North America, the clemency of the climate, the fertility of the land and the nature and availability of local building materials were vital factors which would influence their lives and future prosperity profoundly. The great outdoors dictated not simply the agrarian practices by which many rural communities survived, but also played an important role in defining a host of different regional architectural styles, both inside and out.

Deep in the heart of a verdant Tennessee forest,
dense trees provide a shady backdrop to a veranda.

Above left: Behind an Adirondack-style railing a Lemoyne Star quilt lies on a chair.
Above right: Mailboxes remain unchanged.
Below left: Not only was wood vital for the construction of houses, it was also used as the main source of fuel for cooking and heating.
Below right: Flat walls were achieved by square-hewn logs and remnants were used for fencing.

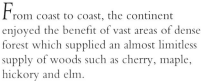

*F*rom coast to coast, the continent enjoyed the benefit of vast areas of dense forest which supplied an almost limitless supply of woods such as cherry, maple, hickory and elm.

From the log cabins of the north and midwest to the clapboard houses and picket fences of the eastern seaboard, wood was a staple and versatile building material. The style of New Englander

homes on the east coast was somewhat subdued and holdings were constrained by the smallness of the plots of land that were available with the purchase grants from the British Crown. In this corner of North America white picket fences sprang up as each settler tried to mark out his small territory from that of his neighbor. While the New Englanders fought to keep themselves warm, farmers in the south were preoccupied with keeping the heat at bay on dog day afternoons. The *Gone With The Wind*-style plantation houses with their langorous porches, handsome verandas and tin roofs – which served to deflect the sun – evolved from modest farmhouses which were expanded by generations of one family as the surrounding fertile plains began to pay dividends.

Above and left: The continent's vast forests yielded an abundance of lumber – pine, ash, birch and maple – for the construction of houses, outbuildings such as barns and sheds and simple picket fences to delineate land.

Left: Fencing could be vertical or horizontal and was often used to enclose livestock.
Right: A sunny deck in Seaside, Florida, is furnished with rustic and Adirondack-style chairs, while at its far end hammocks swing in the breeze.

35

Home on the Range

By the early 18th century America had begun to find its feet as a nation and this self-confidence, together with a sense of national identity, found expression in interiors which showed a pride in local craftsmanship. Although many furniture styles were based on English designs, the American interpretation was unmistakable. The Dutch and Germans who came to Pennsylvania brought with them memories of their folk art traditions and cast about for the materials from which to conjure them. Iron was hand-forged into decorative latches and trivets to protect table tops. Tin was cheap and easy to cut and pattern with punched designs of hearts and songbirds; squares of pierced tin were used for the fronts of pie safes, with the holes serving as ventilation. Furniture – from hefty blanket chests packed with belongings to ingenious Shaker cupboards with smooth-fitting drawers – was almost universally fashioned from wood. And American flora and fauna found their way into textile and stencil designs.

Country homes evolve over the generations; here hand-crafted pine cabinets accommodate modern appliances.

THE KEEPING ROOM

The keeping room was the name given to the main – and often the only – room in early American homes. For pioneers who built themselves shelter in the form of humble log cabins or stone dwellings, the family's living space consisted of a single room on ground level, perhaps with a loft above for storage and for sleeping. Over time, as farmers began to increase their financial wherewithal their homes evolved from these modest beginnings and a second or third room would be added to the original house. Now very much a thing of the past, the keeping room was used for cooking, eating, sleeping and various other household activities. Here, culinary implements were placed on either side of a log fire which was laid on traditional andirons. Bunches of herbs are hung from the

Opposite: The country feel of this keeping room-cum-kitchen or dining room is achieved by a large open hearth, hanging bunches of herbs and other rustic accessories.
Above left: In the traditional manner, a few pieces of furniture have been painted in this room but most of the wood has been left bare.
Above right: The keeping room was the forerunner of the kitchen; here the wall cupboards are painted in a deep colonial red.

beams overhead to dry. The floor of this centralized living area was of rammed earth or stone and would be covered with rushes which were changed once a year. Furniture was equally rudimentary and at mealtimes roughly made stools or benches were pulled up to planks laid over trestles for the duration of the meal.

KITCHENS

The kitchen evolved from the keeping room and its importance as the heart of the home can be traced back through the centuries to the time when meals were cooked on open fires and life was lived within the confines of a single room. Most kitchens adapt well to country style and as such they become the hub of the household and the place for relaxed informality where the table dominates, families are nourished and friends gather together. For most the kitchen is necessarily a 20th-century interpretation of rural reality. However, modern appliances should be discreetly concealed behind cupboard doors. Forgo built-in cabinets in favor of a wooden server and a walk-in pantry.

Above left: A galley kitchen in California with a floral theme.
Above right: A touch of colorful Mexican style blends with cool granite work counters and flagstones.
Left: Old mixing bowls used to store apples and garlic.
Right: A collection of plates hung on painted plank walls.

Open shelves are quite in keeping and provide ideal display space for serving dishes, homey pottery, skillets and culinary receptacles made from copper, pewter, earthenware and wood. Flagstones or plain tiling provide suitable flooring and furniture, for instance, an oak refectory table and a rocking chair, which should be simple and sturdy.

Nothing needs to match, for a unifying theme is more authentic than a dainty dinner service. Seating can be a collection of different styles or woods, perhaps a mixture of Windsors, ladderbacks and banister-back chairs. Forsake electric lighting and decorate the room with arrangements of freshly picked wild or dried flowers and bowls of shiny apples.

Above left: Blanched wooden furniture set against cool, white-stained adobe tiles.
Above right: A homey kitchen decorated with baskets and cornbread molds.
Left: Cast aluminum skillets look at home in any kitchen.
Right: A New England sink made from a slab of granite.

The traditional all-in-one keeping room evolved into the distinctly separate rooms we are familiar with today – while culinary and washing activities shifted to the kitchen, the living room also took its cue from the old single-room country home where "living room" meant just that – part kitchen, part bedroom, part reception room, with all family and domestic activity revolving around the hearth.

As the most public room in the house it is appropriate that heirlooms, antiques or homemade crafts are part of the decor. However, nothing should be too precious or studied, for as a gathering place for family and friends comfort and informality should be the principal ingredients. In cool climates this means a warm cocoon created from overstuffed seating, soft pillows, warm rugs and a roaring open fire. In hotter regions, a refreshing retreat is called for, with light color schemes, ceiling fans, tiled floors and shuttered windows.

As in any other part of the house, an unstructured and, above all, an unself-conscious look is called for. American country style is characterized by engaging mixtures of furnishings, which evolved naturally from a melting pot of diverse immigrant cultures. This feel can be achieved without any great expense and aptly follows the rural tenet of simplicity and making do. Furniture, pictures, fabrics and accessories can be a happy jumble of styles and pieces from different dates and traditions.

Left: A Western or cowboy-style living room composed of natural materials: wood ceiling and floor and river-rock fireplace. Against these hues of stone and wood, color is provided by bright Navajo rugs and Molesworth motifs on the pillows.

Left: In this cosy New England living room a combination of Navajo Indian weavings, colorful patchwork quilts and rag rugs create a welcoming decor. On the right a 19th-century Texas sampler quilt hangs over the back of a hide-covered chair.

Right: A Spanish colonial *santos* or saint's cupboard.
Below left: A very early *kiva* ladder dating from 1800 stands against the wall of this Santa Fe living room.

Below right: In this sunny New England living room well-worn painted furniture is mixed with generous armchairs to give an impression of informal comfort.

As a background to a comfortable and cosily furnished living room the walls may be painted in almost any shade – it is the way that color is applied, in rough, thick strokes with an easy-going attitude to layers of paint and bulging surfaces, which gives that authentic country look. Earth colors such as terra-cottas, ochres, browns and greens all blend successfully with old furniture and wood. And in hotter regions white, cream, pale blues, yellow or a peppermint green, perhaps spiced with a bright, eye-catching hue,

will create an invitingly cool interior. The soft, rich colors of milk paints, which seem to have been mellowed by the years, have a beauty that ready-mixed paints rarely achieve. Appropriate lighting helps to complement the aged and lived-in feel of living-room walls – in addition to low-wattage bulbs placed under simple shades, make use of plain chandeliers, oil lamps, paraffin and storm lamps and perhaps use simple candle holders or tin sconces in order to give supplementary illumination.

Above: The spacious living area of a 1737 Amish farmer's log house which was found in Lancaster County and moved to Chester County. The two-board pegged, yellow pine tavern table, c.1740, is flanked by a pair of ladderback chairs from c.1830 that retain their original brown paint. The sofa is new and upholstered with a checked Delft-color fabric.

BEDROOMS

By the 18th century the days of entire families sleeping en masse in one room were over and the bedroom became an essentially private domain. Until this time only the very rich enjoyed the privelege of such a chamber and most people slept communally, often on the floor of the by-gone keeping room, where they simultaneously lived, cooked, ate and received visitors.

The separate bedroom became a much more hygienic place than before: washable cottons and linens imported from the Far East replaced furs and tapestries, and beds made of cast-iron frames which were less of a haven for bugs, became popular. The mattresses of beds with

wooden head- and footboards rested on ropes which were tightened by turning a number of pegs: this was the origin of the saying "Night, night, sleep tight". Bedding was ample and consisted usually of straw and feather mattresses overlaid generously with blankets and quilts.

Right: A typical late 19th-century Tennessee country bedroom with a four-poster rope bed with a child's trundle bed concealed underneath it and homemade rugs on the floor.
Below left: This wood-panelled bedroom is painted a restful gray-green and the pine floorboards are softened with 19th-century rag rugs. The focal point is the bird's eye maple Sheraton high post bed, dating from c.1800.
Below right: A Seven Stars quilt made c.1850.

Quilts are essential in a country-style bedroom, adding color and a cheerful hominess. As an alternative, a random-patterned, hand-stitched patchwork bedspread will contribute an equally authentic touch. Beds should be simple in style, although this does not preclude a modest form of hanging.

During the 19th century a gentle eclecticism evolved and bedroom decor began to include collections of china ornaments, framed watercolors, painted washstands and floral fabrics. A familiar feature of the room was a sizeable rush or wicker basket with a lid known as a "feather basket" in which down and feathers were gathered for stuffing and plumping up mattresses, bolsters and pillows. Large wooden cupboards and solid, painted blanket boxes or chests also furnished the room.

Whether today's room is furnished with a dressed four-poster or a simple metal-framed bed, polished floorboards or bright, comfortable rag rugs, pretty chintz drapes or bare windows, it will conform to one premise: the country bedroom is never grand.

Ingredients

Choosing the right ingredients is an essential part of creating a successful country style. The roots of the style are found in America's rural past, when practicality and necessity, as oppose to fashion, dictated shape and form. Walls, woodwork, ceilings and floors should form an appropriate framework for furniture, fabrics and accessories. Take your pick of natural colors, from deep earthy tones to pale pastels and apply them to rough-hewn wood or uneven plaster; a distressed look is always preferable to perfect finishes. Then add vegetable-dyed fabrics, painted or mellowed wood furniture and flowers from the local countryside for a harmonious whole. When buying furnishings there is no need to keep to a single period, like the buildings, the elements that make an authentic country-style room tend to span the centuries. You should be aware of tradition, but you need never feel obliged to follow it slavishly. Country is a living style and not a carefully reconstructed slice of the past.

A collection of late 19th-century American patch-work and appliqué quilts displayed in a pie safe.

WOOD

Wood was a rich and universally used natural resource which, with a highly versatile nature lent itself to the widespread construction of walls, windows, doors, floors, furniture and detailing on all kind of domestic items. It might be crudely worked for the structures of houses – logs were often split into wide planks and then placed, in what was known as *puncheon* flooring, so that the flat sides formed the floor of one room and the round sides the ceiling of the one below. As tools and skills developed carpenters and craftsmen turned, planed, polished and fretted wood to produce a host of furniture designs and decorative architectural details which were often a surprising contrast to the severity of the rooms around them.

Typical furniture found in the homes of New Englanders and other settlers

Above: A natural oak stable door complete with iron hinges and latches is set against white milk-painted wall paneling in this late 18th-century American country home.
Right: Details such as hinges, knobs and latches are the key to creating a country interior that still manages to maintain 20th-century conveniences, while at the same time capturing the character of an earlier era. Hand-crafted pine cabinets provide an authentic face while also accommodating modern appliances.

would be a combination of what they had needed for their journey – for instance, traveling chests for holding blankets and china – and simple pieces made on arrival and based on designs familiar from home: the bow-backed Windsor chair for the English and huge wardrobes for the Dutch and Germans.

The Shakers made unadorned and beautifully proportioned tables and benches and cleverly designed serving and sewing counters, desks and chests of drawers which contained the tools and utensils necessary for indoor work. Cupboards and drawers were usually

Above: Whittled wooden coat pegs on the wall of an 18th-century American mud room.
Left: A painted 19th-century chair and a rag rug in the hallway of a red-painted log house.

built-in and some wooden settles were fitted with hinged flaps to convert them into tables. The ladderback chair, with a seat woven from rush or fabric tapes, was the Shaker solution to the need for seating that was sturdy, yet light enough to be hung up out of the way, on wooden pegs fixed onto battens that ran around the room. Through an almost total dependence on wood both function and economy came to the fore in these rustic interiors.

STENCILS

Stenciling is a method of transferring a motif or pattern onto a contrasting colored background by applying paint through cut-outs made in a stencil card.

In North America, during the 18th and 19th centuries, stenciling provided an inexpensive alternative to costly hand-printed wallpapers which were originally imported from Europe. While an ever-increasing choice of wallpapers was easily accessible to town and city dwellers, in rural parts they were either simply not available, too expensive to purchase, or unsuitable for covering wood or plaster walls which were frequently suffering from damp.

On the one hand, stencils became a simple and inexpensive way of introducing color and pattern into the home and designs were often copied from the elaborate interiors of wealthy houses. On the other hand, stenciling was a form of folk art. They were usually executed by itinerant artists and craftsmen from different European extraction, who brought with them a diversity of ideas on decoration from their places of birth. For instance, the flamboyant styles of 17th-century Dutch and 18th-century Scandinavian interiors was reflected in a profusion of hand-stenciled motifs and patterns applied to walls, floors, joinery and furniture in American homes. Applied with milk paint or distemper, the stenciled motifs and patterns were inspired by nature and leaves, flowers, animals and birds were popular. The versatility and engaging simplicity of this decorative technique has seen it flourish to the present day.

Above: The wooden plank walls of this cottage near Houston in Texas were stenciled with a "pattern-box" motif by itinerant German painters at the end of the 19th century.
Right: A bedroom wall is given naive stripes using two alternating stenciled floral motifs. Reconstructed in the American Museum in Bath, England, this is a typical 19th-century American country bedroom.

Above: This Canadian late 18th-century table and kitchen chairs are a delightful example of the appeal of a time-worn painted finish.
Left: A 19th-century clothes press in a bedroom has been decorated with a stain which has then been streaked and grained while still wet.
Right: Folk furniture, such as this brightly painted Mexican cupboard, together with a Jamaican stool, is appropriate for country-style homes.

PAINTED FURNITURE

Wood walls, wood paneling and wood furniture gave interiors ample scope for decorating surfaces with paint.

The colors were used to counterpoint each other – the matchboarding on the walls perhaps painted a blue-green, the door a deep brick-red and a small cupboard a vivid turquoise. This geometry of colors is a hallmark of American rural interiors, inspired by the wealth of trees and the low cost of paints which were home-made from milk and dyed with natural pigments derived from local earth, rust, plants and berries.

Furniture was frequently constructed from inexpensive and inferior woods and then disguised with matte paints in order

Above: An ox-blood colored cupboard.
Below left: A pair of handsome sea chests provide storage space and lend a rustic feel.

to cover the deficiencies of the grain and for the sheer joy of decoration. On some of the most delightful pieces layers of paint are partly worn away to reveal a patchwork of faded colors and raw wood. You can copy this look to improve new pieces by patchily applying different-colored coats on the bare wood; then add an even top coat. Rub the paint with damp wet-and-dry paper to reveal color and grain. Years of continuous use can be simulated by rubbing through to the grain and scuffing and chipping corners and edges.

Above: An elegant contemporary Shaker rocking chair, the back and seat are made of bright red and green woven fabric tape.
Below: Adirondack furniture-makers were known for incorporating organic forms such as twigs and branches in their rustic designs.

Above: A modern Amish chair is perfect for furnishing a country porch or veranda.
Below: White wicker chairs with pillows or squabs are suitable for southern interiors.
Below far right: A simple but sturdy Amish rustic-style chair fashioned from twigs.

depending on the woods that were locally available. The classic rocking chair was invented in the 19th-century south in answer to the need for comfortable seating and would lullaby its occupant to sleep in the afternoon heat. Windsor chairs and settees were found alongside so-called banister-back chairs (the backs were adapted from balusters split in half so that the inside was smooth, for sitting against). In the late 19th century Old Hickory style armchairs and rockers were made from the plentiful Indiana hickory tree; the wood was boiled and bent over metal frames and thin pieces were soaked and then woven for seating.

As with other types of furniture, chair designs were governed by the practicalities of rural life, instead of the passing fashions. English pieces were brought in the holds of the trade ships that stopped along the Atlantic coast for America's cargoes of tobacco and wheat and so rustic versions of Chippendale and Hepplewhite Georgian designs gradually appeared in rural homes during the 18th and 19th centuries. By the same route furniture designed for ships, like the lightweight rattan steamer chair, made its way onto porches and verandas. Although many chairs were inspired by English designs, the adopted styles were simplified and varied considerably from one part of the country to another,

POTTERY

Pottery, whether glazed or unglazed, patterned or plain, has been utilized, collected, handed-down and displayed for centuries. From cumbersome stewing pots to delicate egg cups, pottery finds its true home in the country kitchen. It should be kept on display so that pieces are on hand for practical chores and at the same time lend the room authentic decoration. The kitchen server was designed for exactly this purpose and laden with painted china cups and saucers, jugs and teapots or 19th-century spatterware, it has become a sort of culinary shrine. Likewise, open shelves (or just the top half of a server) provide space for arranging pottery jars filled with cooking implements, salt-glazed brown containers and stoneware crocks for storing flour, sugar and bread alongside bunches of dried herbs, treen or copper molds and rustic baskets. Old kitchen armoires and chicken mesh or glass-fronted cupboards are also ideal for storage and decorative plates make charming wall decoration. You can collect and combine a medley of all types of glazes and patterns: mixing and matching is quite in order.

Opposite: This pottery set, displayed in an old wood server, was produced for a steakhouse by the Wallace company who made hotel and restaurant china from 1938-65.
Above: Unglazed ceramics and stoneware are ideal textures for receptacles in a country kitchen; this *tamali* pot is from Mexico.
Left: Mexican pottery is crudely decorated with naive motifs hand-painted in bright colors. Pieces are rarely perfectly matching, giving it a special charm. Here, the inside of a cupboard is painted a warm red to complement the glassware and pottery housed inside it.

QUILTS

Left: Homemade textiles, in particular colorful quilts, are a principal ingredient of country style. Hand-stitched antique quilts can be attractively displayed and well preserved by folding and then placing them on the deep open shelves of a wood cabinet. *Below:* This North Caroline Lily quilt is made up of a combination of patchwork and appliqué; it was probably stitched in Illinois around 1880.

Early quilts were made from scraps of cloth which were handworked in order to provide warm bedding. At a time when several members of the family commonly shared a single large bed, the quilt would have been quite sizeable.

Even as the communal bedroom developed into smaller, separate rooms and homes also began to incorporate guest rooms, quilts remained a popular form of bed covering. The concentrated labour and skilful needlework involved in the minute stitching elevated quilts above their utilitarian origins and fine examples, for instance, specially worked wedding quilts – showing the names of the bride and groom and the date of the marriage – were much admired.

Quilt patterns evolved in a variety of vernacular styles. The Crazy quilt was made up of all sorts of colors and fabrics. Signature quilts were stitched to raise money for a local church or a school and autographed by signees. And the Bible provided all sorts of decorative motifs such as the Star of Bethlehem, Jacob's Ladder and the Crown of Thorns. Organic patterns were adapted from nature and floral, vegetable and animal motifs were popular. By the late 19th century quilting had achieved the status of folk art and the so-called "best quilt" of the household was so elaborate that it was stitched only during daylight hours, in honor of an important event. Today, best quilts are highly soughtafter and, as they were used sparingly, they have survived in good condition.

Above: Covering an impressive Adirondack-style bed with a domed rustic twig headboard lies a Honeycomb patchwork quilt.
Below: Another Adirondack-style bed with a simpler twig headboard is covered with a Double Nine Patch quilt. Patchwork pillows and a cupboardful of folded quilts complement the bed covering.

Textiles, in particular hand-stitched quilts, patchwork, embroidery and appliqué are the key to recreating a country-style interior. You can mix all sorts of textiles together: in genuine rural homes, furnishings were augmented over the years and each generation contributed to the character of the house, adding layers of memory and tradition.

The textures, patterns and colors of antique textiles juxtapose perfectly with the relatively plain surroundings of stone and planked or log walls. Floorboards can be warmed with painted floorcloths and colorful rag or woven flax rugs, and beds embellished with printed or embroidered covers. For most windows, shutters – sometimes on the inside as well as the outside – will suffice, as only in the grander rural rooms would drapes have been found: lightweight muslin in the summer and heavier cloth for the cold winter months.

The warm hues of native American rugs and blankets complement the rugged furniture of cowboy and Tex-Mex interiors. These may be hung from walls or draped over furniture, banisters, beams, ladderback chairs, *kiva* ladders and even used for upholstery. You should avoid hanging any kind of valued textile in direct sunlight as this causes

Opposite: Beacon blankets were machine-woven between the 1930s and the 1950s. These show various Indian designs and hang over the foot of a cowboy-style cedar-post bed. At the head of the bed is a pile of pillows made from Navajo weavings.

Left: In an Adirondack-style living room a late 19th-century Log Cabin quilt and a Crazy patchwork cushion lie on an armchair.

Below: This so-called "Trigger" bedspread, embroidered in a cowboy theme, was made in the 1940s and covers the back of an old rocking chair, c.1930s, salvaged from a Texan farm.

fading: instead keep them in dappled light so that they retain their original colors. Textiles are especially personal expressions of folk art and are imbued with history. For instance, the early pioneers travelling into the heartland of the New World would bury their dead shrouded in a favorite quilt before continuing on their journey. Then, as now, textiles are prized possessions, fusing the functional and the decorative, and they should be used and displayed as such.

INDEX